and for cleaning your teeth.

We need water to wash our clothes . . .

to cook food, and for making drinks.

You can play with water . . .

and swim in it.

You can use water to blow bubbles . . .

and pour it from one thing to another.

the sea

a stream

a pond

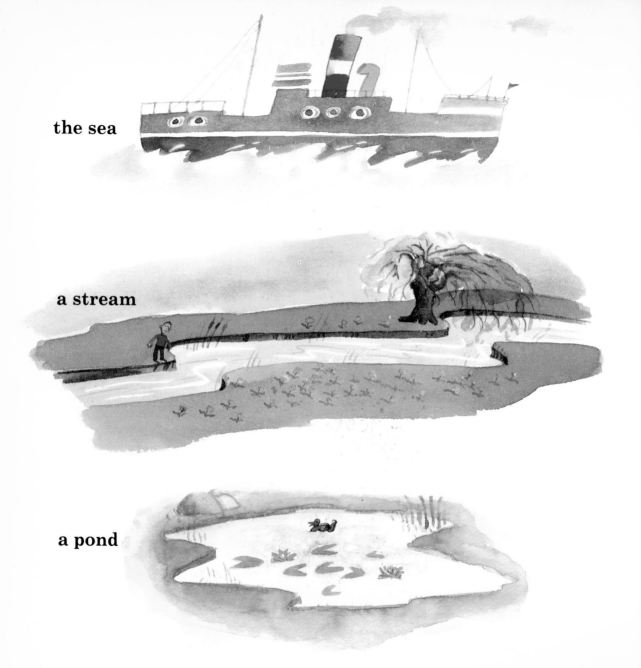

You can find water in all sorts of places.

Outside, water comes from rain.

Inside, water comes from taps.

Some things float on water . . .

others sink.

**Which of these objects do you think will float?
Which will sink?**